SCHOLASTIC

TRUE OR FALSE

Reptiles

BY MELVIN AND GILDA BERGER

TRUE! Dinosaurs were early reptiles.

Today there are more than 8,000 different kinds of reptiles. They are divided into four large groups: snakes, turtles, alligators and crocodiles, and lizards. Most live in warm places. Most lay eggs. And all are cold-blooded. Their body temperature changes according to the surrounding temperature.

Like all reptiles today, dinosaurs had dry, scaly skin.

Some
snakes have
two heads.

TRUE
OR
FALSE?

TRUE! Two-headed snakes are rare, but they do exist.

A two-headed snake lived in a New York zoo around 1900. One head often attacked the other when the snake started to eat. In time, the snake died of starvation. Yet Thelma and Louise, a two-headed corn snake, lived for sixteen years at the San Diego Zoo and produced fifteen normal babies.

There are no snakes in Antarctica, Greenland, Iceland, Ireland, and New Zealand.

Snakes walk on tiny legs. **TRUE** or **FALSE?**

FALSE! Snakes do not have legs.

They crawl about on their bellies. To move forward, snakes form their bodies into S-shaped curves and push off against soil, rocks, or plants. Some snakes can jump up into the air. A number are able to swim — or even climb trees!

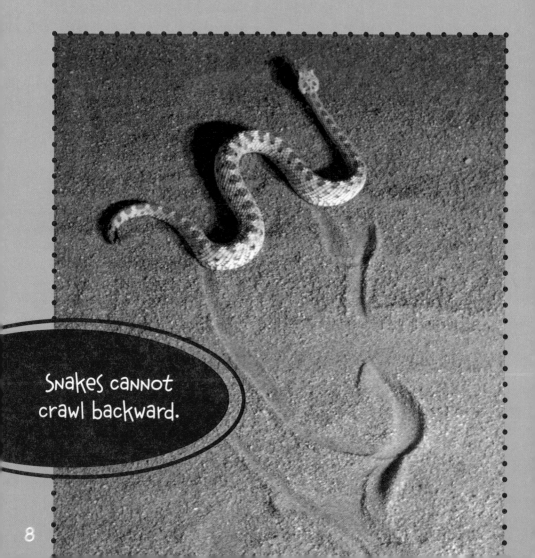

Snakes cannot crawl backward.

A snake can
sting with
its tongue. **TRUE**
OR
FALSE?

FALSE! A snake's tongue is harmless and used for touch.

The snake also sticks out its tongue to pick up scents in the air. Then the snake puts its tongue into a special place in its mouth. This sends a message to the brain, which lets the snake know if something nearby is good to eat.

Some snakes eat only once a year

Snakes are wet and slimy.

TRUE OR FALSE?

FALSE! A snake's body is dry and smooth — never wet or slimy.

Its body is covered with fishlike scales that may be smooth or bumpy. The scales overlap and stretch apart, which lets a snake bend into any position — even coil up into a ball.

As its outer skin wears out, a snake grows a new skin underneath and sheds the old one.

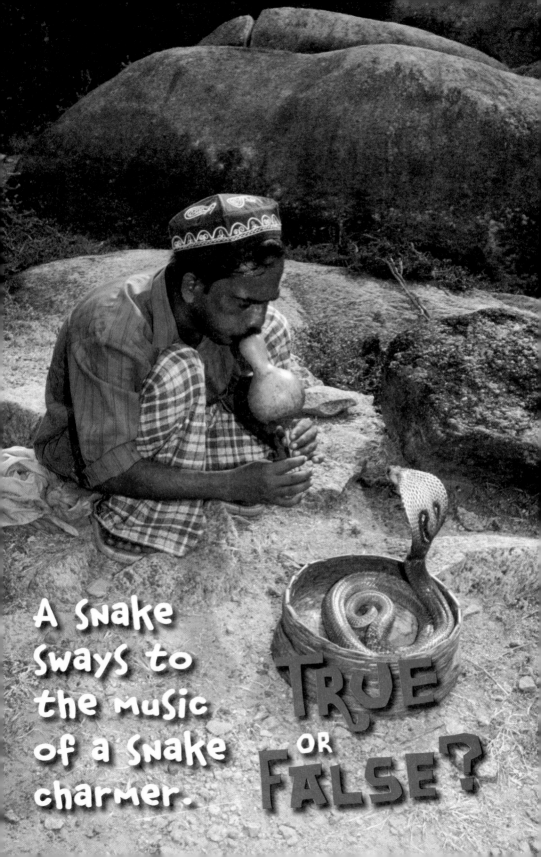

A snake sways to the music of a snake charmer.

TRUE OR FALSE?

FALSE! A snake cannot hear the charmer's music.

A snake just follows the movement of the pipe and the charmer's swaying. The snake slowly raises its head and neck just as it follows any prey — ready to attack. Snake charmers use cobras, which flatten their necks before striking.

Snakes "hear" by feeling vibrations in the ground.

14

All turtles live on land. **TRUE** OR **FALSE?**

FALSE! Only some turtles live on land.

Turtles that live on land are sometimes called tortoises. They are usually found in woodlands, grasslands, and deserts. Freshwater turtles divide their time between land and rivers, lakes, or ponds. Sea turtles rarely leave saltwater oceans and seas. Only the females come on land to lay their eggs.

Turtles are the oldest reptiles on Earth and have changed little in 300 million years!

Turtles are Slow. TRUE OR FALSE?

FALSE! Only land and freshwater turtles move slowly.

A tortoise might take several hours to walk a mile that you can cover in about fifteen to twenty minutes. But sea turtles are not slow at all. A leatherback turtle can swim 22 miles (35.4 kilometers) per hour, more than four times faster than the fastest human swimmer!

Sea turtles have flippers instead of legs to speed them through the water.

Turtles have no teeth. **TRUE** OR **FALSE?**

TRUE! INstead of teeth, a turtle has jaws lined with sharp, hard edges.

The jaws slice through animals or plants like knives through butter. Turtles that live on land mainly eat plants, including grass, leaves, and fruits, plus some insects and small animals. Freshwater and sea turtles feed on sea plants as well as fish, jellyfish, and crabs.

Sea turtles can swallow food only when their heads are in the water.

Turtles have few enemies.

TRUE OR FALSE?

FALSE! Turtles are surrounded by enemies of all kinds, from fish to birds to raccoons to humans.

But turtles' shells offer good protection. When in danger, most land turtles hide inside their shells. They pull in their heads, tails, and all four legs to keep safe from harm.

Turtles can live longer than any animal on Earth.

All turtles hatch from eggs.

TRUE OR FALSE?

TRUE!

Baby turtles are born from eggs the mothers lay on land.

Female land and freshwater turtles dig nest holes in soft ground or even in rotting logs. Sea turtles come out of the water and dig deep nests on sandy beaches. The number of eggs varies from one to hundreds. After laying her eggs, the turtle covers the hole with sand or soil and leaves the nest. The sun warms the earth, the turtle eggs hatch — and the baby turtles dash to safety.

Female sea turtles lay their eggs on the beac where they were born

Alligators look exactly like crocodiles.

TRUE OR FALSE?

FALSE! Just look at their snouts.

Alligators have wide, U-shaped snouts. Crocodiles have narrow, V-shaped snouts that come to more of a point. Also, the alligator's fourth tooth on the lower jaw fits inside the upper jaw when the mouth is closed. The crocodile's fourth tooth is outside its upper jaw.

Alligators only live in the southern United States and eastern China; crocodiles live in Florida, Africa, Australia, Central and South America, Mexico, and Southeast Asia.

Crocodiles make good parents.

TRUE OR FALSE?

TRUE!

Both parents guard the nest where the mother lays her eggs. When the eggs are ready to hatch, the babies call out with loud piping noises. Some mothers and fathers will even help the babies break out of their shells. After the babies hatch, the mother carries the young in her mouth to water. She watches over them until they are ready to live on their own.

Baby crocodiles grow very fast — up to a foot (0.3 meters) a yea until they are around six years old.

Alligators and crocodiles mainly eat fish.

TRUE OR FALSE?

TRUE!

But alligators and crocodiles will eat almost any creature that lives in or near the water. Both alligators and crocodiles have many big, sharp teeth, but they never chew their food. Instead, they use their teeth to grab their prey — any animal from a snake, frog, or turtle to a hog, deer, or cow — and gulp it down.

A human can easily hold an alligator's mouth shut, since an alligator has few muscles to force it open.

Crocodiles sweat when they get hot. **TRUE OR FALSE?**

FALSE! Crocodiles — and alligators — are cold-blooded animals.

They need the sun's heat to give them the energy to move around. That's why they take long naps basking in the sun. But as hot as they get, they never sweat. The large, tough scales on their backs keep them from drying out.

Crocodiles cool off by returning to the water, moving into the shade, or opening their mouths.

When swimming, alligators move their tails from side to side. **TRUE** OR **FALSE?**

TRUE!

Alligators — and crocodiles — swim like fish, by moving their powerful tails from side to side. Often, they float in the water with their legs held close to their bodies. Only their eyes and nostrils stick up above the surface. This makes them look like floating logs and hard to spot.

Alligators and crocodiles prefer shallow water to deep water, and slow-moving streams to fast-moving rivers.

All lizards
are small. **TRUE**
OR
FALSE?

FALSE! Only about 9 out of 10 different kinds of lizards are small.

Small lizards use their long, sticky tongues to grab insects such as crickets, flies, and grasshoppers. But large lizards prey on mammals, birds, and other reptiles, small or large, dead or alive. The biggest lizard of all is the Komodo dragon. An adult male can be 10 feet (3 meters) long and weigh 176 pounds (80 kilograms).

Lizards often capture victims in their mouths and swallow them as soon as they stop moving.

Geckos can walk upside down. **TRUE OR FALSE?**

TRUE!

Geckos have feet with soft, sticky pads at the ends of their toes. Each toe pad has millions of tiny hairs that help the gecko hold on while walking up walls or across ceilings. Some geckos also have hooks that move in and out like the claws of a cat — useful for climbing trees.

A gecko can hold up an object many times its own weight with its toes.

Most lizards are easy prey for enemies.

TRUE OR FALSE?

FALSE! Lizards have many unusual ways of defending themselves.

The small Australian frilled lizard, for example, spreads out a big frill around its head. Suddenly, it looks much larger and scarier than it did before. And, if this is not enough, the lizard opens its mouth — and hisses loudly. That usually works!

Some lizards can break off their tails, which wriggle on the ground while they escape.

Chameleons can change their color. **TRUE OR FALSE?**

TRUE!

OftEN, the color change helps Some chameleons hide from their enemies. But in other chameleons, the change can show shifts in mood. A green chameleon will turn black when it is angry. It turns yellow if it is in danger or under attack.

Chameleons catch insec with the Sticky tips o their long tongues.

The basilisk
lizard can
walk on
water. **TRUE**
OR
FALSE?

TRUE! Basilisk lizards make their homes in riverside trees or bushes.

When threatened, however, these lizards jump into the water. They then get up on their back legs and start running across the surface, moving so quickly and lightly that they do not sink or drown.

The basilisk has huge back feet.

Some reptiles make good pets.

TRUE OR FALSE?

TRUE! Some reptiles are very friendly.

But reptiles, like all other living beings, need excellent care if they are to survive and grow. They have to get the right kinds of food and living conditions to stay healthy. There's much to know before attempting to care for a pet snake, turtle, or lizard at home or in school.

Reptiles are among the world's most beautiful, varied, and interesting animals.

Index